the neglected Spirit

Understanding and Adoring the Holy Spirit

Pastor Mike Novotny

Published by Straight Talk Books
P.O. Box 301, Milwaukee, WI 53201
800.661.3311 · timeofgrace.org

Copyright © 2017 Time of Grace Ministry

All rights reserved. This publication may not be copied, photocopied, reproduced, translated, or converted to any electronic or machine-readable form in whole or in part, except for brief quotations, without prior written approval from Time of Grace Ministry.

Scripture is taken from THE HOLY BIBLE, NEW INTERNATIONAL VERSION®, NIV®. Copyright © 1973, 1978, 1984, 2011 by Biblica, Inc. ® Used by permission. All rights reserved worldwide.

Printed in the United States of America

ISBN: 978-1-942107-31-6

TIME OF GRACE and IT ALL STARTS NOW are registered marks of Time of Grace Ministry.

Contents

Introduction 4

Holy Spirit 101 5

Different Parts, One Purpose 17

Turn Right! 29

Conclusion 41

Introduction

For being equal with God the Father and God the Son, the Holy Spirit doesn't seem to have an equal place in most Christians' lives. Sure, Christians confess that they believe in him, but what role does the Spirit play in their daily lives?

The Bible has thrilling and almost-too-good-to-be-true things to say about the Holy Spirit. The Spirit is the key to faith, love, joy, and peace, realities that every Christian (and every human!) deeply longs to find. What we all crave in our hearts are the exact gifts the Holy Spirit longs to give us!

Best of all, Jesus promised that our Father loves to give the Holy Spirit to those who ask him (Luke 11:13). If parents enjoy giving gifts to their children, how much more will the perfect Parent (God) smile as he gives us a gift better than anything this world has to offer, that is, the Holy Spirit?

Therefore, I invite you to join me in exploring the passages that open our eyes to some of the most important, yet most neglected, teachings in the entire Bible—the glorious person and the life-changing work of the Holy Spirit. I pray these truths move you to love the Holy Spirit just as much as you love the Father and Jesus, the Son.

Holy Spirit 101

If you enjoy awkward silence, you should come to my Bible 101 class, because the beginning of lesson 5 is always awkward. That's when I say, "Tell me everything you know about the Holy Spirit."

"Uh . . . well . . . in the name of the Father and of the Son and of the Holy Spirit. I believe in the Holy Spirit, the holy Christian church."

"Is he (is it?) like a dove? Or like fire? Like a dove on fire? Like the *Hunger Games*? Hungry for God?"

"Can we go back to the Jesus lesson?"

Most people just sit there in awkward silence. After one class, a guy told me, "I feel bad for the Holy Spirit. He does all this work and no one remembers him."

What about you? Do you know the Holy Spirit? Do you love him, talk to him, invite him, worship him, remember him? Most Christians don't. Pray to the Father. Worship the Son. And forget the Holy Spirit. But we can't forget the Holy Spirit. Here's why—

> "I feel bad for the Holy Spirit. He does all this work and no one remembers him."

because some of us are worried, worried about finding a job, paying rent, getting chemo, having chronic pain.

And some of us are scared. Scared for our son who doesn't believe in Jesus. Scared we won't know what to say in spiritual conversations. Scared she'll never come back to God.

And some of us are struggling. Struggling to have a marriage built on mutual submission. We know "you first" makes us blessed, but "me first" is what we've both been doing for a long time.

And some of us feel "less than." Our happiness disappears in the land of "Er" when we see a skinn*er* girl, a funn*ier* guy, a health*ier* friend, a smart*er* classmate. We compare all day long, and that envy rots our bones.

And some of us doubt—we doubt God could forgive us, accept us, love us, or like us.

Do you know what all of those issues have in common? The Holy Spirit can fix them. Trust instead of worry. Faith instead of unbelief. Sacrifice instead of sin. Contentment instead of comparison. Grace instead of guilt. That's exactly what the Holy Spirit wants to do.

And that's why I wrote this book—to get us all thinking about knowing and loving the Holy Spirit. To talk to him, pray to him, follow him, keep in step with him, listen to him, love him, worship him. This section is a crash course on the Spirit: Holy Spirit 101. I want to teach you the *who*, the *what*, and the *how*. Who the Holy Spirit is, what the Holy Spirit does, and how the Holy Spirit does it. Ready?

Who is the Holy Spirit?

Check out this diagram. Isn't our God amazing!

This is what Christians call the triune God, or the Trinity. *Triune* is Latin for three-in-one—because there are three separate persons (Father, Son, and Spirit) but only one God. I know that's a mystery that doesn't fit in my 3-pound brain, but that's what God's profile picture says. But here's what I want you to remember: if there are three persons, then the Holy Spirit is a . . . *person*. Brilliant, I know.

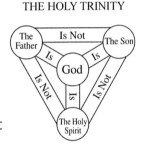

THE HOLY TRINITY

And because he's a person, he has a *personality*! In fact, search the Bible for the Spirit and you'll find a whole list of words that describe him.

The Spirit leads us, guides us, teaches us, convicts us, speaks to us, comforts us, gives to us, strengthens us, equips us, and about 30 other verbs. Think of the best leader you've ever worked for. Think of the best teacher you've ever learned from. Think of the most compassionate friend you have. The Holy Spirit is like that, but better.

In addition, you can resist the Holy Spirit, grieve the Holy Spirit, quench the Holy Spirit. You can block his calls, ignore his texts, and lock the door of your heart. What you did to your ex or your enemy, you can do to the Spirit. Because God the Holy Spirit is a person with a personality!

> Search the Bible for the Spirit and you'll find a whole list of words that describe him.

The Spirit is like Sam's roommate. Sam had never met anyone like his college roommate, Hewson. Hewson was the happiest guy Sam had ever met. He was relentlessly optimistic and bursting with ideas. Sam loved hanging out with Hewson. Whenever Sam wasn't sure about a decision, Hewson knew what to say. When Sam was worried about his brother's cancer diagnosis, Hewson put him at ease. When Sam was close to a debt-inducing Amazon binge, Hewson snapped him out of it.

But things weren't always so easy. When Sam vented about his chemistry professor, Hewson called Sam out for gossiping. Annoyed, Sam stormed out of the dorm . . . but the more he thought about it, the more Hewson was right. Something about Hewson made Sam feel . . . content, at peace. Hewson pushed him, but it was always toward love.

Does that sound like anyone you know? The Holy Spirit, maybe? There's this famous blessing in the Bible that says, **"May the grace of the Lord Jesus Christ, and the love of God, and the fellowship of the Holy Spirit be with you all"** (2 Corinthians 13:14). *Fellowship.* Because the Holy Spirit is a fellow, a person, with the most magnetic personality. So, treat him that way. Talk to him. Ask him questions. Call out to him. Invite him. Pray to him. He's a person, after all. That's who the Holy Spirit is.

God the Holy Spirit is a person with a personality!

But what exactly does the Holy Spirit do?

Read the apostle Paul's words to the Corinthians: **"You know that when you were pagans, somehow or other you were influenced and led astray to mute idols"** (1 Corinthians 12:2).

Here's what the Holy Spirit does—he keeps you from idols. That was definitely true for the Corinthians. Back in Corinth, people worshiped at the temple of Apollo—the god of music, healing, and truth. They worshiped at the temple of Aphrodite—the goddess of love, pleasure, and fertility. The Corinthians used to be influenced by those temples, those mute statues. They sacrificed for them. They sinned for them. But that was then. "You *were* pagans," Paul says, until the Holy Spirit showed up.

The Spirit does the same thing today. In our culture, we don't see too many obvious idols. No, our idols are undercover. They're good things that turn into god things (and that's a bad thing!).

Think of something like Control. If Control is your idol, you need to be in control—your list, your way, your schedule. You need to know what's happening. You need to make the final call. You can't handle not getting your way. You get worried and stressed and grouchy. You don't delegate much. You don't trust God's plans. Everyone in the room knows you're going to push to get your way.

Or maybe your idol is Comfort. If Comfort is your idol, you'll sin to be comfortable. You'll spend for your present comfort and save for your future comfort, but you won't give uncomfortably generous amounts. You'll scroll through your phone instead of helping out. You'll watch the game instead of playing with your kids. You'll extend the afternoon on the boat even if you miss church.

Maybe your idol is Attention. If Attention is your idol, you'll sin to be noticed. You'll talk too much.

You'll make perverse jokes if people laugh. You'll grab the mic and tell the stories that make you look impressive.

Somehow or other we are influenced and led astray to these idols. But that's what the Holy Spirit changes. The Holy Spirit opens our eyes to see how bad that is. He convicts us of sin. The Holy Spirit teaches us the dangers of trusting in idols. "They'll fail you!" he shouts. "You'll end up stressed, annoyed, pressured to impress. They can't give you peace. They can't fill you with joy."

> The Holy Spirit teaches us the dangers of trusting in idols.

And then the Holy Spirit does this: **"Therefore I want you to know that no one who is speaking by the Spirit of God says, 'Jesus be cursed,' and no one can say, 'Jesus is Lord,' except by the Holy Spirit"** (1 Corinthians 12:3).

The Holy Spirit turns us to Jesus. He teaches us, enlightens us, fixes us on these three words: *Jesus*—The Son of God. Born of a virgin. A perfect life. Gave his life for my idols, for my sins. *Is*—Not "was." Jesus is not a past tense; remember him? No, he still is. Risen from the dead. Triumphant over death. With me always. Ruling the universe for his church, for me. *Lord*—My ruler. My master.

Absolute power, absolutely no corruption. He is faithful and forgiving and good. That's the Holy Spirit's agenda—to fix your eyes on Jesus.

Have you heard the news about Michael Phelps? He's the Olympic swimmer with the 8-foot arms and 23 gold medals. He's the most decorated Olympian in human history. Rio was his fifth Olympics, and he dominated in it. But did you know Michael Phelps almost killed himself? Two years ago, after winning more gold medals than he had fingers, Phelps felt empty. He was struggling to figure out who he even was. Success was his idol, but the idol couldn't satisfy his soul.

He turned to heavy drinking, got his second DUI, and got caught by a tabloid with a bong in his hand. The idols of pleasure failed him, broke him. So he thought there was no reason to live. "I thought the world would be better off without me," Phelps admitted. Thankfully, he didn't die but ended up in a treatment center in Arizona. That's where a friend gave him a book about God, about purpose, about something way better than a few gold circles. And it saved him. The joy filled him up so much that he told everyone in rehab about it. They nicknamed him "Preacher Mike."

That's what the Holy Spirit does. He takes people who are pursuing empty idols and turns them to Jesus. "You want attention," the Spirit says. "People are fickle. That won't work. How about the attention of God? Because of Jesus, God is watching over you, noticing you, appreciating you. You want control? How about the control of God? There is nothing—no twist, no turn, no surprise, no tragedy—that he does not use to mature and bless and draw you closer to him. So, put down the remote and live with the peace of knowing God's got this. You want comfort? How about comfort of the soul? How about living with a clean conscience, washed by the blood of Jesus? How about

> He takes people who are pursuing empty idols and turns them to Jesus.

letting go of shame, knowing you matter because God loves you? How about the green pastures and the quiet waters of believing the Lord Jesus is your Shepherd?" Turning us from idols to Jesus—that's what the Holy Spirit does!

But how does the Holy Spirit do it?

Peace that lasts. Joy that doesn't disappear by Tuesday. I want that. We want that. But how do we get it? How does the Holy Spirit turn us to Jesus? Now that's a big question. How does the Holy Spirit teach and guide and convict and comfort? With a whisper? a feeling? an intuition?

Let me answer that massive issue with three passages. Romans 10:17 says, **"Faith comes from hearing the message."** The Holy Spirit gives faith in Jesus. How? Through the . . . message. In John 17:17, Jesus prayed, **"[Father], sanctify them by the truth; your word is truth."** *Sanctify* means to set apart as holy, to set apart from idols. And how does that happen? By the Word. Second Timothy 3:16,17 adds, **"All Scripture is God-breathed and is useful for teaching, rebuking, correcting and training in righteousness, so that the servant of God may be thoroughly equipped for every good work."** Every good work. Every last thing the Spirit wants you to do. So what did the Holy Spirit breathe out to equip you? All Scripture.

Get the point? The Bible, which is the book the Spirit inspired. Why? So he could talk to you. So you wouldn't have to guess if that feeling was God or just gas. So you wouldn't have to wonder if that was the Spirit talking or Satan deceiving. "The heart is deceitful," the Spirit wrote. So don't listen to your heart; listen to the Word. That's how the Holy Spirit has promised to do his amazing work of creating and strengthening your faith. Here's the big idea: the Spirit uses the Scriptures to point you to the Savior. Spirit. Scripture. Savior. Wind. Word. Worship. That's how the Holy Spirit works.

There once was a small village with an old well

in the center of the grass-roofed huts. The well didn't look all that impressive, but for generations it kept the village alive. The water from that well quenched the thirst of hundreds over the years. It kept little ones alive and refreshed tired bodies after long days in the fields. So every day the villagers stopped at that well and drank. Until one day, a traveler came walking up the dusty road.

"You could have better," he told the villagers. "Just over those hills I found water. Crisp water like I had never before drank. If you follow me, I'll show you." The villagers looked at each other, shrugged, and agreed. For hours they walked, until it was dark. Their mouths dried up and their tongues stuck to their cheeks. But on the traveler hiked. "Right here," he promised. "Right here is where I found the water. It sprung up from the ground." But all the villagers saw was dry ground.

"We should pray," the traveler insisted, "pray for God to send fresh water." So they prayed. And they waited. And they wished they were back at the well that always gave water (story adapted from the book *The Fire and the Staff* by Klemet Preus).

Get it? What if we changed that story. What if the village was the church, the water was the

> *The Spirit uses the Scriptures to point you to the Savior.*

Spirit, and the well was the Word? You see, there is a reliable place to find the Spirit. And it's not up in the hills of feelings. It's right in the Word. Sure, it's been around a long time. But the Bible has been the Spirit's way of giving faith for thousands of years. It's why he inspired it, so you could read it and quench the thirst of your soul in the promises of Jesus.

You know who the Spirit is—a person. You know what the Spirit does—turns us from idols to Jesus. And you know how the Spirit does it—through the Bible he inspired. So what now? What if we added a prayer? Before your quiet time with the Word, what if you prayed to the Holy Spirit?

> The Bible has been the Spirit's way of giving faith for thousands of years.

"Holy Spirit, I need you. I need you to teach me today. Expose my idols. Equip me with your promises. Open up the heavens. I want to see Jesus. Help me persevere, to read until you teach me, until I get it. Holy Spirit, you wrote it. Now teach it. Amen."

Different Parts, One Purpose

We've talked about who the Holy Spirit is, what he does, and how he does it. But those truths might leave you with a cookie-cutter impression of the work of the Spirit—same Spirit, same job, same tools to get the job done. But look around and you will soon find out that God's people are not at all the same. That is why we need to explore how the Spirit uses different people to accomplish his one mission—to bring us closer to God. So, are you ready to figure out how you are so different from the people around you? I hope so, because it is one of the keys to being truly Spiritual!

We're all different. Have you ever thought about how different we all are? Think about your friends or coworkers or fellow church members. Who's an extravert? Who's an introvert? Who's athletic? Who's artistic? Who's type-A organized? Who's a free spirit?

Married people, have you ever taken that *5 Love Languages* quiz? Isn't that the worst? "Honey, you got Acts of Service. If you just changed to Physical Touch, I really think our marriage would be stronger . . ." But people are different. I potty-trained my firstborn with candy and my second with summer sausage (true story). People are different. Take the StrengthsFinder test, Myers-Briggs Type Indicator, or the DISC profile assessment, and you'll find out people are different.

But different is dangerous. Because differences are the leading cause of what I'm going to refer to as OCD—Obsessive *Comparison* Disorder. Only about 1 percent of Americans have actual OCD (Obsessive Compulsive Disorder), but I think 99 percent of Christians obsessively compare themselves to others.

Just watch what happens to your heart when you detect a difference between you and someone else. OCD leads to pride and/or envy. You might feel pride puffing up inside:

"Why don't you just trust God like I do and stop worrying?"

"What's so hard about talking to people? I do it all day."

"Why are you so focused on your to-do list? Relax like I am."

"Why don't you just give like the Bible tells you to?"

"Am I the only one who volunteers around here?"

"You don't read books? It's not that hard."

"I don't get why you make such dumb choices."

"You seriously don't see the problem with your way of thinking?"

Or you might feel envy rotting your bones:

"I wish I could do that."

"I wish I got that award."
"Look at how pretty she is."
"Look at how much attention he gets."
"See how many likes she got."
"He got the raise."
"She got the job."
"They got noticed."
"I can't sing like that."
"I can't make people laugh like that."
"Why can't I do anything that matters to God?"
That's the envy of OCD.

Once we start to compare our gifts, our abilities, our bodies, our intellects, our athleticism, our artistry, our success, our failures, our families, our metabolisms, our lives—something ugly happens. OCD happens. And it rips us apart. It destroys the unity of a family, a class, a team at work, even a church.

> Watch what happens to your heart when you detect a difference between you and someone else.

But the Holy Spirit wants better than that for us. The Holy Spirit wants to produce the fruits of love and joy and peace and kindness and gratitude and contentment. He wants you to know how to deal with the differences you'll notice this week. That's why he led a pastor named Paul to write down the antidote to OCD.

I bet many of you have heard of this part of the Bible. Ever been to a Christian wedding and heard, "Love is patient. Love is kind. It does not envy. It is not proud"? You might assume that passage is about two hand-holding lovebirds. But it's not. It's actually about two fist-raising groups at a church.

The first-century church at Corinth was fighting. The problem? An OCD outbreak. You see, some members of the church had impressive, attention-getting, even miraculous gifts. They could heal sick people, speak in languages they never studied, and work miracles with their bare hands. They were like the big biceps in the body of Christ. But others felt like the armpits. All they could do was serve and show mercy—wash the dishes after the church picnic or hold the hand of a dying relative. Guess what happened? OCD. "Do we have to do everything around here?" the first group wondered as they healed another sickness. "Do we even do anything around here?" the second group sighed as they dried another plate.

So the Spirit told Paul to write about love. But before those famous words, "Love does not envy. Love is not proud," he told them the antidote to their OCD. Check it out: **"There are different kinds of gifts, but the same Spirit distributes them. There are different kinds of service, but the same Lord. There are different kinds of working, but**

in all of them and in everyone it is the same God at work" (1 Corinthians 12:4-6). Different gifts. Different service. Different workings. Paul says that we're all different. And that's a good thing! In fact, he chose the word *gift* intentionally. It comes from a word that means "grace," or "undeserved love." Your differences are all grace. You didn't deserve them. God gave them to you as a gift. God wanted your gifts to be different.

But the Holy Spirit wants better than that for us. The Holy Spirit wants to produce the fruits of love and joy and peace and kindness and gratitude and contentment.

That's why Paul brings up the Trinity. Did you catch that? **"The same Spirit . . . the same Lord** [that's Jesus] **. . . the same God** [that's the Father]**."** There is just one God, perfectly united, yet there are three different people—the Father, the Son, and the Holy Spirit. And they do different things. The Father didn't die on a cross. The Spirit didn't rise from the dead. Jesus did. But do you think the Trinity has OCD? Do you think Jesus is proud when the Trinity has waffles in the morning? "Dad, could you pass the butter with those hands that weren't pierced for the sins of the world?" Do you think the Holy Spirit envies Jesus? "All those guys down there with cross tattoos, and I get to be a dove? No dude wants a dove!" No! The Trinity is filled with love and praise. The Holy Spirit is a happy Spirit when people praise Jesus. The Father loves it when we love his Son. The Son adores it when we adore the Spirit. They are best friends, perfectly content, despite their differences.

That's what God wants his kids to do too. Paul continues, **"Now to each one the manifestation of the Spirit is given for the common good"** (1 Corinthians 12:7). This is a key verse. To each one. Of the Spirit. For the common good. Think of it like this. Imagine a gift that's labeled like this—To: Each one. From: The Holy Spirit. For: The common good. We might say this gift is to you, from him, for them. Different gifts, same giver, same goal. You might be a natural leader. Not everyone is. Where'd that come from? The Spirit! And here's his goal: Do good with it. Lead people toward God. Lead a service team at church.

Or maybe you have the gift of encouragement. You care about people and think about them a lot. Where did that come from? The Spirit. Here's his goal: Do good with it. Send a daily text to someone who needs some courage. Reach out to someone and encourage him or her with your prayers.

Or maybe your gift is knowledge. You love to

read, listen, and learn. Not everyone does. Where did that come from? The Spirit! And here's his goal: Do good with it. Soak up the podcasts, books, blogs, and share your knowledge. Send a top five takeaway list to your team. Start a conversation at dinner and share the point of your latest podcast.

Our gifts are different, but the same Giver gave them for the same goal—to do good!

Our gifts are different, but the same Giver gave them for the same goal—to do good!

That's what Paul told the Corinthians: **"To one there is given through the Spirit a message of wisdom, to another a message of knowledge by means of the same Spirit, to another faith by the same Spirit, to another gifts of healing by that one Spirit, to another miraculous powers, to another prophecy, to another distinguishing between spirits, to another speaking in different kinds of tongues, and to still another the interpretation of tongues. All these are the work of one and the same Spirit, and he distributes them to each one, just as he determines"** (1 Corinthians 12:8-11).

Lots of people get distracted by the fancy gifts on this list. But that's not really Paul's point. If you compare this list to the lists of spiritual gifts in Romans chapter 12, Ephesians chapter 4, and 1 Peter chapter 4, you'll find almost zero overlap. Same topic, different gifts. So it appears that the main point is not to give us this list of gifts so we can figure out which one we have. What you will find in common is that every list gives the antidote to OCD. Romans 12:3 says, **"Do not think of yourself more highly than you ought."** Ephesians 4:2,3 says, **"Be completely humble. . . . Make every effort to keep the unity of the Spirit."** Peter says, **"Each of you should use whatever gift you have received to serve others"** (1 Peter 4:10). The point is to fight pride and envy and division and to let our differences delight us, not divide us.

The goal is to glorify God for giving this body such different gifts.

All of that is squeezed into this two-word phrase: "spiritual gifts." It's the cure to both pride and envy. Pride's cure is to remember spiritual gifts are . . . gifts. God just gave them to you. You didn't beat everyone at the playground race because you had a personal trainer. God gave you athleticism. Studies came easy because God made you that way. You can't be proud about a gift.

And envy's cure is to remember spiritual gifts are . . . spiritual. They're from the Holy Spirit. And if there's one thing I know about the Holy Spirit, it's that he's holy! He's pure and perfect and good. So whatever gift he gave you, it has to be good. He doesn't make mistakes. He doesn't spite people or rip them off. He handpicks the perfect gifts. So why would I envy what the Holy Spirit didn't want to give?

Let's practice. I have a mailbox like everyone else I know. Except mine's in a bucket because my neighbor ran it over . . . about four months ago. Yeah, that's right, four months ago. It took me about a month to get the bucket out there and another month to buy a new mailbox. I tried a few weeks later to set it up, but it was leaning like an Italian tower.

Can you guess what my gift *isn't*? But can I tell you what my gift is? Memorization. This month I've been killing it. My new record—125 passages memorized in a month. Boom! Now, I wonder what you're thinking right now? Is your OCD kicking in? Is pride whispering, "Four months? Dude, it's a mailbox not a trip to the moon. It's not that hard"? Is envy groaning, "125 passages? I haven't memorized that many in my life. I stink at being spiritual"? This is why Paul says, "Different gifts! You love to fix things because of a gracious gift. I love to memorize because of a gift of grace." The goal is not to compare. The goal is to glorify God for giving this body such different gifts.

That's why Paul gets "bio-logical." Listen to his logic in 1 Corinthians 12:12, **"Just as a body, though one, has many parts, but all its many parts form one body, so it is with Christ."** Different parts! One body, but different parts! I love my wife's eyes, but I'm glad she's not a giant eyeball. I love my daughters' little toes, but it would stink if they were just toes (get it?). And this is why we call ourselves church members or members of a family. It's not like being a Costco member—you pay us an annual fee and then you do whatever you want. No, *members* also means *parts.* That means when you are a church member or a member of the family, you are a valuable part. We need your gracious gifts. And you need ours. Put us all together and this body of Christ can do some incredible things. The antidote to OCD is to shout, "Different parts!"

Let me give you four next steps to becoming more (holy) spiritually gifted.

1. Learn your gifts. Figure out how the Holy Spirit made you. Take a Strengthsfinder test and a *5 Love Languages* quiz or just think about what you love to do (and what you never get

around to). Thank the Holy Spirit for making you you!

2. Leverage your gifts. Use your gifts for the common good. If you are good with kids, how can you serve kids? If you are a great hostess, when can you get people together? If you have the gift of generosity, could you try to double your giving? If you have the gift of service, there's this mailbox on my street that's been sitting in a bucket for four months . . . okay, that was shameless. But seriously, do you want the address?

3. Love their gifts. Ax the OCD and praise people for their gifts. "When you sing, it helps me worship Jesus." "You have a way of pushing me to get better at my job." "Thanks for coaching my kids. I don't know how you have so much patience."

4. Look to God's gift. Look to the gospel of Jesus.

We learned what the Holy Spirit does. He turns us from idols to Jesus. And that, honestly, is the antidote. Why do you envy? Because you think if you'd only be like him or her, you'd be somebody. But here's the thing—*you are somebody*. Jesus gave his life so you would always be somebody. Because of Jesus, angels are applauding for you. Because of Jesus, the Father notices you. Because of Jesus, your work is never useless, never pointless, never in vain. Sure, that guitar gets him the girls. But you have God! Yeah, his personality wins him awards. But you have eternal awards in heaven. They have a condo in Hawaii. You have a mansion in paradise. She has one million fans. You have one marvelous Father.

If everything you need, everything your heart really craves, is found in Jesus (and it is), then you can deal with the differences. Envy won't rot your bones. Pride won't puff you up. Your heart will be at peace. And when OCD starts to itch at your heart, you'll look up to Christ, the head of the body, and smile, "Different parts!"

Turn Right!

Do you ever do stuff you don't want to do? I do. Last summer I had my final soccer game of the season. And my goal all summer had been to be a missionary for Jesus, to invest in people and invite people and evangelize people with the best news in the world. To be respectful to the ref, cool to my opponents, generous to my teammates. I prayed before games: "God, my goal is not goals. It's you. I don't want to win. I want to worship you." And I was doing pretty well . . . until the last game. It was getting heated, things got chippy, the ref missed a call, they tied it up with a few minutes to go, I got the ball up close to their goal, and I . . . well, I didn't exactly take a dive, but I fell down like a gentle petal. Sure, I got bumped, but not pushed hard enough to fall (especially in the closing minutes of a tie game). The ref pointed to the spot. Penalty kick. The other team protested violently. I said nothing. We scored. We won. But I lost. "Nice dive," the other team muttered. Nice dive? Nice work, Mr. Missionary. Way to make a great impression for how Christians live. And the whole way home I thought, "I didn't want to do that."

Ever been there? Have you ever been at the stop sign of choices with a chance to choose what's right or what's left and you turn the wrong way (again)? Maybe you promised yourself you'd behave at the party, but then the guy you like asked to get you another drink. Maybe you promised God you would bite your tongue with your ex, but then he pushed your buttons like only he can. Maybe you swore you were going to be a more selfless husband, but then you felt so rejected sexually. Maybe you were really going to stick with the Bible reading this time, but then work got crazy. Maybe you told yourself, "Don't compare! Different parts!" but then they promoted someone younger with less experience. It happens with interrupting, with overreacting, with worry, with whining, with porn, with pride, with everything. We do the stuff we don't want to do.

And that's why we need the Holy Spirit. We need the Spirit to make us more spiritual, to help us choose to walk with God instead of away from him. But how does that work? What should we do?

That's what the apostle Paul wants to tell us. Check out Galatians chapter 5: **"So I say, walk by the Spirit, and you will not gratify the desires of the flesh"** (verse 16). If you don't want to gratify the flesh (that sinful part of your heart), then walk by the Spirit. Where the Spirit walks, you walk. Where the Spirit turns, you turn. Do that, Paul says, and you won't do the stuff you don't want to do.

But, Paul admits, that's not so simple. Because

the flesh is . . . well, the flesh. **"For the flesh desires what is contrary to the Spirit, and the Spirit what is contrary to the flesh. They are in conflict with each other, so that you are not to do whatever you want. But if you are led by the Spirit, you are not under the law"** (Galatians 5:17,18). The flesh is a stubborn, unteachable, arrogant bully. All it wants is a fight. And you can't change its mind. You can't teach your Old Adam new tricks.

> We need the Spirit to make us more spiritual, to help us choose to walk with God instead of away from him.

In every Christian heart, there is something evil, something ugly, something that wants to grab the Spirit, rip out his feathers, cut out his tongue, and toss his mangled body in a ditch.

Imagine it this way: There's a red ribbon of sin that wraps around your heart, runs down to your fingers, and reaches up to your thinking. It infects and affects every single decision that you make. It makes angry fists and cowardly feet and unfair assumptions easy, no YouTube tutorial required. And this hates the Spirit. This wants to sin. This craves and longs and lusts for it.

Think of it this way: Imagine your life is like driving down spiritual streets. God is down that road to the right. Sin is down that lane to the left. And every second of the long, long trip, the flesh is navigating. "Turn here!" "Oh, I know a way better way than that." "We NEED to stop here. You'll love it." Sin's begging, pleading, pushing, promising, deceiving, lying, telling only the short term. And that's why it happens. That's why we struggle.

But if we don't struggle; look where the flesh will take us: **"The acts of the flesh are obvious: sexual immorality, impurity and debauchery; idolatry and witchcraft; hatred, discord, jealousy, fits of rage, selfish ambition, dissensions, factions and envy; drunkenness, orgies, and the like"** (Galatians 5:19-21).

Here's what that list means: Sexual immorality is any sexual activity outside of marriage: porn and masturbation, premarital sex, sexting, staring, lusting. Impurity and debauchery is dirty sex without restraint—Mardi Gras or bachelor party kind of sin. Idolatry is loving a false god, praying to Buddha, or trusting your own opinion instead of God's. Witchcraft is turning to spiritual forces that don't come from the Spirit—horoscopes, spells, palm readings, tarot cards, etc.

Hatred is when you want to see someone suffer. A rival embarrasses herself. An ex's relationship fails. A critic gets criticized. When your heart is happy about that, you hate. Discord, dissensions, and factions are tension-filled relationships. The third graders who won't invite her to play. The 30-year-olds who have a clique at work. Jealousy and envy are when you feel bad because they're better. You resent his success or the attention she gets. Fits of rage are when you go off—one bad driver, one dumb political ad, one word in the wrong tone and—boom!

Selfish ambition is when your goals are all about you. You study math or practice piano or work 60 hours/week because you have goals that, honestly, have little to do with God. Drunkenness is when you are filled with spirits instead of the Spirit, when others notice you acting differently when you drink. Orgies are what rap videos depict and what every pic-clicking porn user is a part of. And that's in you! That's in me! That evil, ugly, vile thing is in our hearts. And it's still in the car, screaming, "Turn left! Turn left!"

> That evil, ugly, vile thing is in our hearts. And it's still in the car, screaming, "Turn left! Turn left!"

But here's the worst part: **"I warn you, as I did before, that those who live like this will not inherit the kingdom of God"** (Galatians 5:21). Paul's not playing. If this is how you live, you won't see God. The original Greek here doesn't mean a slip or a sin I keep doing and keep hating. No, it means a lifestyle. This is what you do and what you plan to do. If that's you, it's proof that you don't have the Holy Spirit, because the Spirit would hate that. He'd be in conflict with that. But some of you don't fight. And if that doesn't change, you will go to hell. I know that's a bit of brimstone and fire, but I'd rather warn you about the fire than watch you walk into it.

I can't help but think of her—someone I care about, someone going down a bad path. She knows it. She admits as much in my office. And before I open the Book and quote the Spirit, she knows what I'm going to say. What she's doing is not right. But to her credit, she still talks to me, still listens. The other day she asked, "So, do you think I'm going to hell?" But it doesn't matter what I think. It matters what God says. And he says you can't shove the Spirit out of your heart and be a spiritual person.

> *If you walk by the Spirit, if you turn toward what's right, you'll be on that road.*

But there's a better road than the highway to hell. There is a path to God, a path that ends in eternal life, a path that blesses even here and now.

If you walk by the Spirit, if you turn toward what's right, you'll be on that road. Paul writes, **"But the fruit of the Spirit is love, joy, peace, forbearance, kindness, goodness, faithfulness, gentleness and self-control. Against such things there is no law"** (Galatians 5:22,23).

The fruit of the Spirit is what the Spirit produces. When the Spirit isn't gagged in the trunk but sitting shotgun, there are snacks the Spirit shares. There are streets he inspires you to travel. Like *Love*. When people do what's best for each other, no matter who, no matter what, that's love. Or when boyfriends who care about dating God's way also care about your reputation and about your feelings. And *Joy*. That's a good feeling deep in your soul that makes you happy even when life is sad. "I'm sick but I'm still loved by God." And *Peace*. Peace is the happy thought, "God's got this! My Dad runs the universe, so I'm not freaking out about who runs our country." And *Forbearance*. That's a fancy word for *patience*. Patience is when little things like flooded basements and messy rooms don't become big things in our hearts. And *Kindness* and *Goodness* and *Faithfulness* and *Gentleness*. People with these attitudes are just fun to be around; they make you feel better after you talk to them. And *Self-control*. This is the ability to say no to the flesh. "I'm not going to say that." "I'm not going to do that." This is walking by the Spirit.

Not only does the Spirit want you to see God face-to-face in heaven. He also wants you to enjoy the ride. So he brings what every good road trip has: snacks. Lots and lots of snacks. The fruit of the Spirit.

There are two ways to live, two roads to choose. The flesh is to the left, and the Spirit to the right. But back to our original question—*How?* How do we actually do the stuff we want to do? Well, here's Paul's answer: **"Those who belong to Christ Jesus have crucified the flesh with its passions and desires. Since we live by the Spirit, let us keep in step with the Spirit"** (Galatians 5:24,25). That's it. If you want to keep in step with the Spirit and live by the Spirit, don't forget this: *you belong to Christ.* If you keep your eyes fixed on this, fixed on him, you'll turn right.

Once upon a time there were a bunch of bickering men on a church leadership team. A long history of too many harsh words and too few apologies made for major tension at every meeting.

The pastor wasn't sure what to do. He knew these men believed in God, but they kept giving in to the flesh month after month. Nothing seemed to change, until the pastor had an idea. He brought a big circular table into the meeting room. Then he found the largest cross in the church and set it upright in the middle of the table. Finally, the pastor put out name tags on each chair. When the men arrived, they found their assigned seats. And they noticed that those with the most tension were sitting directly across from each other. So when the discussion got heated, when they were *this* close to doing what they always did, the men looked across . . . and saw a cross. In the reflective gold of that cross, each man could see himself. The sight stopped one man in the middle of his sentence, giving the pastor just enough time to quote, "Those who belong to Christ have crucified the flesh." It was hard to forget about love when you were staring right at it.

You belong to Christ. If you've turned from your sin and trusted in the cross, then despite all the sin, all the struggle, all the wrong turns, you belong to Christ. You are his. You don't belong to the flesh. No, you are a child of God. This is your identity. It's who you are. This is where the Spirit first leads you as a Christian—to a new identity.

I am forgiven. I am as holy as the Holy Spirit. I

am as pure as Jesus. My sin has nothing to do with how God sees me. I'm good with God because of the work of God's Son and the faith given by God's Spirit. That's who I am. Yeah, I did that again. I know; I said that again. But when I lie down, I don't belong to that sin. I am not defined by that sin. I am defined by Jesus.

> This is where the Spirit first leads you as a Christian—to a new identity.

Has that thought gripped you yet? You belong to Christ. Some of us struggle with Christian guilt. We believe in Christ, but we just feel guilty all of the time. The flesh keeps shouting from the backseat (he's crucified, not driving after all) and we keep listening. And we still feel unworthy, ashamed, even after we've said sorry to God. But Paul is saying, "Here's the fact: You belong to Christ." God's not thinking about what you said last night. Jesus isn't replaying the footage of your sin, shaking his head. The Holy Spirit isn't whispering about you to all the angels at the watercooler. No! You are not under the law. The law you broke is not hanging over your head or bearing down on your spiritual shoulders. No! Jesus took that pressure off. You are under grace. It defines you, because Jesus defines you. So, Christian, enough with the guilt. Enough of thinking about you. It's time to think about Jesus. You belong to him.

That's where the power comes from. That's what compels you to tell the flesh to take a hike. That's what helps you not do today what you did yesterday. Maybe we could say it this way, "When flesh and Spirit start to fight, think of Christ and then turn right." Cheesy? Perhaps. But I hope it helps.

Could the same thing work for us? When you're frustrated on the field, when you can think of a thousand words to wound, when your parents are driving you crazy, when the flesh really wants an extra glass of wine, when your passions and desires are pleading with you to turn left, what if you remembered Jesus? "I belong to Jesus." Meditate on his love, his sacrifice, and sin will be too weak to make you turn left.

A professor once told me about the easiest choice he ever had to make. He had

It's time to think about Jesus. You belong to him.

been dating his future wife for a while and got invited to her parents' cabin. He was talking to her parents, but she walked into the room. Light purple cardigan sweater. Hair that shimmered like a shampoo commercial. Hearing him tell the story, you would have thought she entered in slow motion! And as he stared at her beauty, she asked him a question, the easiest question he had ever been asked. She smiled, "Do you want to walk with me?"

> Walk by the Spirit and you will not gratify the desires of the flesh.

That's it. Friends, if God is beautiful to you, if he is compelling and big and strong and glorious and good, then when the Spirit smiles and says, "Do you want to walk with me?" you won't have to think. It'll be what you want. So, walk by the Spirit and you will not gratify the desires of the flesh.

Conclusion

Well, do you love him a little bit more than before? I hope so. The Holy Spirit is worthy of our worship and our praise for all that he is and all that he is doing in our lives. Specifically, he is worthy for all that he has done in our hearts!

My prayer is that your heart would leap the next time you hear his name. At a baptism—in the name of the . . . Holy Spirit. At the opening of a church service—We begin in the name of the . . . Holy Spirit. During a devotion where the capital *S* "Spirit" grabs your attention. In those moments, I hope you remember the thrilling truths we discovered.

About the Writer

Mike Novotny has served God's people in full-time ministry since 2007 as a pastor in Madison and now Appleton, Wisconsin. He also serves as a speaker for *Your* Time of Grace video devotions and contributes to the written resources of Time of Grace Ministry. Mike loves seeing people grasp the depth of God's amazing grace and unstoppable mercy. His wife continues to love him (despite plenty of reasons not to!), and he often prays that Jesus would return before his two daughters are old enough to date.

About Time of Grace

Time of Grace is for people who want more growth and less struggle in their spiritual walk. The timeless truth of God's Word is delivered through television, print, and digital media with millions of content engagements each month. We connect people to God's grace so they know they are loved and forgiven and so they can start living in the freedom they've always wanted.

To discover more, please visit timeofgrace.org or call 800.661.3311.

Help share God's message of grace!

Every gift you give helps Time of Grace reach people around the world with the good news of Jesus. Your generosity and prayer support take the gospel of grace to others through our ministry outreach and help them find the restart with Jesus they need.

Give today at timeofgrace.org/give or by calling 800.661.3311.

Thank you!

Notes